YOUR LEGACY

BIBLE STUDY

THE GREATEST GIFT

DR. JAMES DOBSON

developed with Michael O'Neal

LifeWay Press®
Nashville, Tennessee

Published by LifeWay Press®
© 2014 Siggie, LLC

Your Legacy: The Greatest Gift © 2014 by Dr. James Dobson. Published by FaithWords;
A division of Hachette Book Group, Inc.; New York, NY. Used by Permission.

No part of this book may be reproduced or transmitted in any form or by any means, electronic or
mechanical, including photocopying and recording, or by any information storage or retrieval system,
except as may be expressly permitted in writing by the publisher. Requests for permission should be
addressed in writing to LifeWay Press®; One LifeWay Plaza; Nashville, TN 37234-0152.

ISBN: 978-1-4300-3290-8
Item: 005650404

Dewey decimal classification: 249
Subject headings: FAMILY \ SPIRITUAL LIFE \ GENEALOGY

Unless indicated otherwise, all Scripture quotations are taken from the Holman Christian Standard Bible.
Copyright © 1999, 2000, 2002, 2003, 2009 by Holman Bible Publishers. Used by permission. Holman
Christian Standard Bible® and HCSB® are federally registered trademarks of Holman Bible Publishers.

To order additional copies of this resource, write to LifeWay Church Resources, Customer Service,
One LifeWay Plaza, Nashville, TN 37234-0113; fax 615.251.5933; phone 800.458.2772; order online
at *www.lifeway.com* or email *orderentry@lifeway.com;* or visit the LifeWay Christian Store serving you.

Printed in the United States of America

Adult Ministry Publishing, LifeWay Church Resources, One LifeWay Plaza, Nashville, TN 37234-0152

Contents

WEEK 1

WEEK 2

WEEK 3

WEEK 4

About the Author

DR. JAMES DOBSON is the founder and president of Family Talk, a nonprofit organization that produces his radio program, "Dr. James Dobson's Family Talk." He is the author of more than 50 books dedicated to the preservation of the family, including *The New Dare to Discipline; Love for a Lifetime; Life on the Edge; Love Must Be Tough; The New Strong-Willed Child; When God Doesn't Make Sense; Bringing Up Boys; Bringing Up Girls; Head Over Heels; Dr. Dobson's Handbook of Family Advice;* and recently, *Your Legacy: The Greatest Gift.*

Dr. Dobson served as an associate clinical professor of pediatrics at the University of Southern California School of Medicine for fourteen years and on the attending staff of Children's Hospital of Los Angeles for seventeen years in the divisions of Child Development and Medical Genetics. He has been active in governmental affairs and has advised three United States presidents on family matters.

In 1967 he earned his PhD in child development from the University of Southern California and holds eighteen honorary doctoral degrees. In 2009 he was inducted into the National Radio Hall of Fame.

Dr. Dobson and his wife, Shirley, reside in Colorado Springs, Colorado. They have two grown children, Danae and Ryan, and two grandchildren.

MICHAEL O'NEAL is minister of education and missions at First Baptist Church, Cumming, Georgia. He has also served as youth minister, worship leader, associate pastor, church planter, and college/ seminary professor. He and his wife, Carrie, are parents to two boys.

How to Use This Study

The four sessions of this study may be used weekly or during a weekend retreat. But we recommend that before you dig into this material, you watch the film, *Your Legacy* from the *Dr. James Dobson Presents: Building a Family Legacy* film series. This will lay the groundwork for your study. Or consider using the film as an option to extend or conclude this study.

This material has been written for a small-group experience, for you and your spouse, or for personal study.

CONNECT: The purpose of the introductory section of each session invites and motivates you to connect with the topic of the session and with others in your group.

WATCH: The study DVD contains four DVD clips which include introductions from Ryan Dobson and clips from a talk by Dr. James Dobson, based on the film and the accompanying book *Your Legacy: The Greatest Gift* by Dr. Dobson (FaithWords; ISBN 978-1-4555-7343-1.)

ENGAGE: This section is the primary focus of each week's group time. You and other participants will further engage the truths of Scripture and discuss accompanying questions. This section also includes a Wrap Up portion, which concludes the group session and leads to the Reflect section.

REFLECT: This at-home study section helps you dig deeper into Scripture and apply the truths you're learning. Go deeper each week by reading the suggested chapters in the book *Your Legacy: The Greatest Gift* and completing the activities at the end of each session in this study.

Guidelines for Groups

While you can complete this study alone, you will benefit greatly by covering the material with your spouse or by interaction with a Sunday School class or small group. Here are a few ways to cultivate a valuable experience as you engage in this study.

PREPARATION: To get the most out of each group time, read through the study each week and answer the questions so you're ready to discuss the material. It will also be helpful for you and your group members to have copies of the book *Your Legacy: The Greatest Gift* (ISBN 978-1-4555-7343-1). Read it in advance of the study to prepare, and encourage your members to read the corresponding chapters each week. In your group, don't let one or two people shoulder the entire responsibility for conversation and participation. Everyone can pitch in and contribute. In your group, don't let one or two people shoulder the entire responsibility for conversation and participation. Everyone can pitch in and contribute.

CONFIDENTIALITY: In the study, you will be prompted to share thoughts, feelings, and personal experiences. Accept others where they are without judgment. Many of the challenges discussed will be private. These should be kept in strict confidence by the group.

RESPECT: Participants must respect each other's thoughts and opinions, providing a safe place for those insights to be shared without fear of judgment or unsolicited advice (including hints, sermons, instructions, and scriptural Band-Aids®). Take off your fix-it hat and leave it at the door, so you can just listen. If advice is requested, then it's okay to lend your opinion, seasoned with grace and offered with love.

ACCOUNTABILITY: Each week, participants will be challenged to live a life of intentionality and leave a legacy that honors the Lord. Commit to supporting and encouraging each other during the sessions and praying for each other between meetings.

Introduction

Have you ever felt unsettled after reading an obituary or attending a funeral? Have you watched the media cover a noteworthy leader's accomplishments, only to wonder how much time he was able to carve out for his wife and children? Or whether spiritual issues motivated and guided his actions?

Degrees, awards, promotions, wealth, international recognitions—none of these matter for eternity. Only a transforming, passionate, personal relationship with Jesus Christ is abiding.

Years ago, I attended a funeral service for a well-known man. I listened as people shared much about his accomplishments, but nothing about his relationship with God, his passion for Jesus, or the difference he sought to make in order to build the kingdom of God. And nothing was said about the faith of his children. *How very sad*, I thought.

I began asking: *Lord, what will people say about me at* my *funeral? Will they say that I earned a degree or that I was a man of God? Will they say I primarily wanted to promote my reputation or that I desired above all else to promote your great name? Will they say that I chose to climb the ladder of personal success or that I sought to make a difference for You even when I did not receive the praise or see the outcome?*

The answers to these questions will determine the kind of legacy you and I will leave. While we cannot control what future generations will become, you and I are responsible for our own actions and decisions. Will we seek forgiveness for our wrong decisions, will we ask the Lord to continually redirect our hearts to depend on Him, and will we influence others—especially our progeny—to live in a God-honoring way?

It's for certain that you will leave a legacy. The question we will explore in this study is: *What kind of legacy will you leave?* On this four-week journey, we will look at what it takes to build a legacy of faith that honors God and impacts future generations for His glory.

Throughout history, God has involved people in His work and He still is looking for faithful people to use. The Bible tells us, "For the eyes of Yahweh roam throughout the earth to show Himself strong for those whose hearts are completely His" (2 Chron. 16:9). God wants you to be wholeheartedly surrendered to Him, trusting His plan for your life, and He wants to use you in marvelous ways.

He wants you to leave a lasting legacy of faith.

Are you willing? Are you ready? If so, let's get started. I'm on the journey with you!

WEEK 1

DEEP
IMPACT

● **BEFORE YOU BEGIN,** get acquainted with your group and pray together. Ask God to strengthen each family's godly influence on future generations.

> Name someone who has made a lasting impact on you (coach, teacher, parent) and describe the characteristics that made this person special.

> In what ways did he or she influence you?

> Fifty years from now, what would you like your children, grandchildren, and friends to say about you?

Legacy is what future generations recall about you. You are a patriarch or a matriarch and your children, grandchildren, and great grandchildren will take what you have done with your life and build on their own lives. It is the continuation of your ministry and influence (both positive and negative) beyond your lifetime, reflecting what you value and what you believe is important.

Scripture is full of examples and instructions that teach us how to build and leave a legacy of faith.

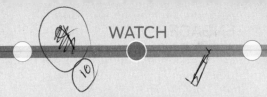

How many stories have you shared with your kids x fan?

PASSING STORIES GENERATION TO GENERATION

● **WATCH CLIP 1** from the study DVD and answer the following questions:

Thank you for joining me in Placid, Texas—the community that shaped the life and ministry of my great grandfather, George Washington McCloskey.

> Think back to the community where you were raised. Describe the town. What are a few memories you have?

> How did the people of that place shape you?

> Have you ever thought much about the legacy you would like to pass on to your family? If so, what do you imagine it would look like?

> What does the word, "legacy," mean to you?
>
> *Military Service?*

The purpose of this group experience is to show you that it is possible to leave a legacy of faith that lasts, one that honors God and makes a difference for all eternity.

● **CONTINUE YOUR GROUP TIME** with this discussion guide.

Thousands of years ago, God interrupted life for the biblical patriarch Abraham. Not only did God capture his attention, He also invited Abraham to embark on a massive journey of faith. Abraham's response to his defining moment would change the world forever.

> Have you ever had a personal defining moment like Abraham's? A time when you believed that you were being asked to make a huge alteration to the trajectory of your life? How did you respond?

Before we dig into Genesis 12 where this story occurs, it's important to know what preceded this turning point, in chapters 1-11.

GENESIS 1-2: The world was in perfect harmony. God had created people in His image to worship, serve, and live for Him.

GENESIS 3: Adam and Eve rebelled against God. Sin, evil, and death—disrupting the perfect relationship between God and His creation—were the consequences.

GENESIS 4: Adam and Eve's older son, Cain, killed his brother, Abel.

GENESIS 6-8: God sent a global flood of judgment against sin.

GENESIS 9: Even after a fresh start, Noah fell away, just as Adam and Eve had.

GENESIS 11: Characterized by selfishness and pride, God's people began leaving Him out of their lives. They build a giant tower to make a name for themselves.

Chapters three through eleven are pretty dark and depressing. And just when there seems to be no hope, plan, or future, there is a turning point. As you look at verses from Genesis 12, pay close attention to God's instruction and Abraham's response.

● **READ** Genesis 12:1.

Nation and family were central to Abraham's social and economic life. But God approached Abraham and commanded him to leave the only life he had ever known to go to a land he didn't know.

> What would you be thinking if you were Abraham?

● **READ** Genesis 12:2-4.

God promised to make Abraham's name great. God kept His promise, as He always does.

> According to verse 2, what was God's purpose in blessing Abraham?

> How has God blessed you? How can you use those blessings to bless others?

> How do you trust God's promises when they do not make sense or do not include the details you would like to have?

God promised to use Abraham to bless the world, even though Abraham didn't know how significant the fulfillment of that promise would be. (See verse 3.) Likewise, God's plan for our lives is greater than we can dream or imagine.

> How does this truth motivate and encourage you?

After hearing God's promises, how did Abraham respond?

Abraham obeyed and God multiplied Abraham's descendants into a great nation. From this family came the promised Messiah.

● **READ** Hebrews 11:8-12.

How do these verses describe faith?

Abraham was an ordinary, sinful person just as we are. But he and Sarah trusted God and lived by faith, anticipating the fulfillment of His promises.

What does Abraham's example teach you?

Just as God invited Abraham to take a courageous journey of faith, so does He invite you to step out and follow His leading.

● **READ** Romans 4:20-21 aloud and ask God to give you this type of unwavering faith:

> He [Abraham] did not waver in unbelief at God's promise but was strengthened in his faith and gave glory to God, because he was *fully convinced* that what He had promised He was also able to perform (italics added).

THIS WEEK'S INSIGHTS

• • •

- A person with faith like Abraham's is fully convinced that God will accomplish what He has promised.
- Abraham obeyed God and God blessed him beyond expectation.
- In his obedience, Abraham gave glory to God and helped establish a legacy of faith for future generations.
- God continues to bless and use people of faith to bless others and give glory to Him.

What next step might God be calling you to take? Consider these possibilities:

☐ If you are not a Christian, He is always seeking you. You can confess your sinfulness and surrender your life to Him and His plan for you.

☐ Be baptized to show others the change Jesus has made in you.

☐ Join a church close to your home. We grow by surrounding ourselves with other people who love the Lord and by serving within the body of Christ.

☐ Begin to pray and study the Bible each day in order to know God more intimately.

☐ Volunteer to serve in your church and use your God-given gifts.

☐ Go on a mission trip and partner with others to meet the world's physical and spiritual needs.

WRAP UP

• • •

PRAY TOGETHER for insight into how God is at work in each group member's life, perhaps creating a defining moment out of ordinary situations. Ask God for faith in His reliability and for the willingness to go whenever and wherever He calls.

● **READ AND COMPLETE** the activities for this section before your next group time. For further insight, read chapters 1 and 2 in *Your Legacy: The Greatest Gift.*

PASSING THE BATON

Relay races are usually won or lost in the transfer of the baton. A critical moment occurs when the runner races around the final turn and prepares to hand the baton to the next runner. If either fails to complete a secure pass, their team usually loses the race.

So it is with the Christian life. When members of one generation are committed to the gospel of Jesus Christ and are determined to finish strong, they rarely fumble the baton. But getting the handoff securely into the hands of their children can be difficult and risky. It may not be the fault of the parents; sometimes young runners refuse to reach out and grasp the baton. Either way, failing to transfer the baton of faith to our children is tragic.

Our story: George and Alice McCluskey, my maternal great-grandparents, had two daughters, Bessie and Allie. Both gave their hearts to the Lord on the same night and, in time, each married a preacher. Bessie and Allie had five children between them, four girls and one boy. All four daughters married preachers, and the son became one. My great-grandfather's daily prayer—that every member of four generations would be believers—was being answered year by year.

On my father's side of the family, God dramatically intervened in the life of my grandfather, Michael Vance Dillingham ... he was known as MV. After his first wife's death, he became embroiled in a bitter dispute with his former brother-in-law, perhaps over a gambling debt. One night MV set out with a gun to kill his brother-in-law. Standing in the shadows, he paused to listen to a brush-arbor revival meeting— and heard the gospel for the first time.

Never intending to stop that night, MV was moved by the Holy Spirit to pause, to listen, and received eternal life instead of taking a life. In front of other worshipers, he took his gun and placed it on the altar. He shared how he knew he was forgiven and a child of God. MV no longer felt anything but love for the man he had planned to kill.

Miles away, George McCluskey and his wife were doing everything they could to win people to Christ. George heard about MV's conversion at the brush arbor *he had built years ago for revival meetings*. George invited Michael to preach and sing at his revival meeting, and ultimately my great-grandfather and grandfather joined forces in a common cause, serving Christ together for years.

MV Dillingham fell in love with George and Alice's oldest daughter, Bessie. After a five-year courtship, they married, establishing my bloodline. With no formal training, "Little Daddy" and "Big Mama" went into communities to preach, often without invitations or lodging and certainly without promise of pay. When food was not provided, they fasted and prayed.

This couple served ten pastorates from 1908 until 1944, when MV died. Their churches grew rapidly and people responded to the simple truths of the gospel. So far, every member of two generations was not only a believer in Christ, but also either a preacher or married to one.

How was the baton of faith passed to you? How do you see God weaving your story for His glory?

mom and MBI on the radio, Catholic Sunday school but they made sure there was a presence and a sign of importance to them, which was unwavering

Identify people in several generations who have made a spiritual impact on you. If possible, let them know of your gratitude for their contribution to your life.

B - DR GOLDBERG
- GRANDMA AHSEN
- Aunt Lorena + Uncle Dick
- Mom (and Dad)

YOUR PART IN A GLOBAL PLAN

By faith Abraham obeyed God, but he did not live to see the complete fulfillment of God's covenant. God permitted His people to be enslaved in Egypt for many years, but He did not forget about them. Eventually, they made it to the land God had promised, and became a nation. God's promise was being fulfilled, but He wasn't finished.

● **READ** a prophet's words centuries later, in Isaiah 42:5-8. What do these verses say about who God is?

HE IS THE SOURCE OF ALL

God's promise to Abraham was less about territories and more about a Savior who would descend from his line. (See Matt. 1:1.) The Messiah would come so all people would know the one true God. Jesus did come to earth. He lived a sinless life and then died in our place and rose from the dead. Before He ascended back to His Father, Jesus gathered His disciples together and commanded them to bless the world.

● **READ** Matthew 28:18-20 and Acts 1:8.

Two thousand years after Jesus commissioned His disciples, thousands of people become believers in Jesus every day. And now, you are working through a Bible study because of the moment when God told Abraham, "I'm going to bless you so that you can bless not just your family, or a nation, but the world."

List ways God has blessed you and ways you might bless others as an overflow of gratitude for His blessings to you.

WAYS GOD HAS BLESSED ME	WAYS I CAN BLESS OTHERS
- SALVATION - GIVEN ME A THIRST FOR HIS WORD	TALK ABOUT JESUS ACT / SERVE BECAUSE OF JESUS

Commit to reach out in love to somebody in your family this week. Be intentional, and make your blessing something special. One of the best ways is to spend quality time with individual family members. Be ready to share a highlight of your experience with your group.

LEGACY SPOTLIGHT: BILLY GRAHAM (BORN 1918)

No person has shared the message of Christ with more people than Billy Graham. Dr. Graham was the first global evangelist, taking the good news of Christ to billions of people through crusades, television broadcasts, radio programs, and print resources. According to a recent Gallup survey, Billy Graham has been among the 10 most admired men in the world for 56 years, finishing number 4 in 2012.[1]

Billy Graham's son, Franklin, is an evangelist and CEO of the Billy Graham Evangelistic Association (BGEA). Will Graham, Franklin's oldest son, is also an evangelist with the BGEA. Recently, Franklin and Will discussed a few lessons they learned from Dr. Graham.

LESSON 1: Love the Bible.
Franklin said, "One of the things my father did at home was to establish devotions every morning and evening. My family started that practice and now my married children do that with their children."[2]

LESSON 2: Spend time on your knees.
When Dr. Graham sat down with Will, he shared that one of his greatest regrets was—surprisingly—not enough prayer. He explained: "When I look back, [I realize] we could have accomplished so much more if we had spent more time on our knees."[3]

Having seen him and other family members practice these spiritual habits over the years, Franklin and Will are convinced that Bible reading and prayer are the two primary ways to express their reliance on God.

"What my Granddaddy was teaching me is to be totally dependent on God," Will said. "Reading God's Word and praying keeps us dependent upon God because we realize that this is never about us. There's nothing we can do to help anybody or to save anybody. It's all God."[4]

> Does your family value Bible reading and prayer like this? It's a tangible way for you to pass along the legacy of faith. If not, what could you do to begin to establish these essential habits?

PERSONAL REFLECTION
• • •

Could what is said of Abraham in Romans 4:20-21 be said of you and your faith today? Why or why not?

UNWAVERING → so wish that was me!!

God's Word should always encourage you to trust God and His promises. As you follow His leadership this week, pray that He will grow your faith in Him.

1. Frank Newport, "Hillary Clinton, Barack Obama Most Admired in 2012," *Gallup* (online), 31 December 2012 [cited 25 June 2014]. Available from the Internet: *http://www.gallup.com*.
2. Ariel R. Ray, "Franklin Graham Reflects on Lessons From Billy Graham in Father's Day Video," *The Christian Post* (online), 20 June 2011 [cited 25 June 2014]. Available from the Internet: *http://www.christianpost.com*.
3. "Will Graham - 2 Lessons from Billy," *Billy Graham Evangelistic Association* (online), 8 March 2011 [cited 25 June 2014]. Available from the Internet: *https://www.youtube.com*.
4. Ibid.

WEEK 2

LIFE

CHANGE

· ·

● **START YOUR GROUP TIME** by discussing what participants discovered in their Reflect homework.

God interrupted Abraham's life, captured his attention, and invited him to take a huge step of faith.

> Share how God has blessed you and your family recently.

> Describe an action you took to bless your family during the past week. What was the response?

As Christ-followers, we experience two kinds of defining moments. The first is our salvation, when we surrender to Jesus Christ, repent of our sin and turning to follow Him. Then as we grow in our relationship with Him, He speaks to us, both gently and dramatically.

This week, pray for God to make you sensitive to His voice, and that you will be aware of God's working to bring new believers to faith in Him.

● **WATCH CLIP 2** from the study DVD and answer the following questions:

God often uses circumstances, both good and bad, to get our attention and to help us realize our need for Him. Today's film clip highlights a clear defining moment in my grandfather's life.

BRUSH ARBOR

What circumstances did God use to capture my grandfather's attention?   *HE WAS CONVICTED OF HIS SIN*

How was my grandfather changed that night?
HATRED WAS REPLACED BY LOVE
HE WAS CALLED TO PREACH

God used a preacher at a revival service to lead my grandfather to surrender his life to Jesus. God used preachers to influence other members of my family. God used my parents, grandparents, and church leaders and members to faithfully tell me about Jesus Christ and make clear my need for a Savior.

Who did God use to lead you into a relationship with Jesus Christ?

How did Jesus change you when you surrendered your life to Him?

● **CONTINUE YOUR GROUP TIME** with this discussion guide.

When you truly allow God to take charge of your life, He makes you a new creation (2 Cor. 5:17). He changes your heart, your perspective, your goals, and your relationships.

In Acts chapter 16, several people, with their families, experienced dramatic change. Paul, Silas, Timothy, and Luke had been traveling from city to city, teaching about Jesus—that He died and rose again, and that forgiveness was available to all who believed in Him. God led them to an influential city called Philippi. A woman named Lydia and a jailer, among others, were glad they came.

● **READ** Lydia's story in Acts 16:11-15.

Lydia, a prominent business leader in Philippi, worshiped God and believed in prayer, but she had not yet become a follower of Christ. There are "religious" people today, too, who may worship and pray, but not know Jesus personally.

> What is the difference between having religion and having a love relationship with Jesus Christ?

> According to verse 14, who opened Lydia's heart and gave her the desire to respond to Paul's message? Why is it important to recognize that only God can change hearts?

The Bible tells us that before we become Christians, we are spiritually dead. (See Eph. 2:1.) Dead people can't do much, can they? If we are spiritually dead, we don't have the power or ability to become spiritually alive. We are not being thrown a life preserver. We are dead on the bottom of the ocean. Only God has the power to give us life.

What does verse 15 tell us about how Lydia responded to Paul's message?

Lydia took three actions, according to this verse:

1. She was baptized. Her willingness to be baptized was a public witness to the difference Jesus made in her life.
2. She committed herself to other believers. She invited Paul and Silas to her house, and at other times hosted Christians in her home. (See Acts 16:40.) Her hospitality and commitment to other Christians demonstrated life change.
3. Lydia led other family members to commit their lives to Christ. Verse 15 tells us that everyone in her household was baptized.

How can one family member influence other family members to follow Christ?

Unfortunately, some city officials in Philippi did not appreciate the work Paul and Silas were doing in Jesus' name. They had the apostles beaten and thrown in jail.

● **READ** the jailer's story in Acts 16:25-34.

What important question did the open prison doors prompt the jailer to ask? How did Paul and Silas answer him?

How did the jailer respond?

The jailer needed and wanted to be saved. He also wanted his family to be saved. He invited them to hear the good news about Jesus.

Who in your family needs to hear the good news about Jesus?

What can you do to share more about Jesus and the gospel?

The pattern of attending church as a family remains an important influence in children's lives. According to LifeWay Research, an estimated 67 percent of adults say they would consider a family member's invitation to worship or Bible study to be an effective approach.[1]

Who might you consider inviting to attend Bible study or worship with you?

THIS WEEK'S INSIGHTS

• • •

- There is a difference between religion and a personal faith relationship with Jesus.
- Only God can change hearts; we cannot change ourselves.
- When we fully surrender to Jesus Christ, He produces life change in our decisions and our relationships.
- God also seeks to change us as we walk daily in faith.

God is also constantly at work in the small moments, inviting us to take new, unfamiliar steps of faith with Him. Wherever you live, work, and play this week, watch for those small, defining moments He places in your path.

WRAP UP

• • •

THIS WEEK, make prayer a priority. Focus on God's amazing grace and Jesus' sacrificial death on the cross and His resurrection. These made your salvation possible. Spend a moment meditating on 2 Corinthians 5:15: "And He died for all so that those who live should no longer live for themselves, but for the One who died for them and was raised."

God, I cannot change myself. I acknowledge that You alone have the power to change me from the inside out. Here I am. Make me more like Jesus today. Amen.

READ AND COMPLETE the activities for this section before your next group time. For further insight, read chapters 3 and 4 in *Your Legacy: The Greatest Gift.*

GOD'S IRREPRESSIBLE CALL

Our story: When he was a baby, my father was dedicated by a highly respected minister, Dr. Godby. When Jimmy Dobson was brought to the altar and placed in the minister's arms, he said, "This little boy will grow up to preach the gospel of Jesus Christ all over the nation." There were no other ministers in the Dobson family, and my father learned of this prophetic word only after he was grown.

At age six, my father told his family he wanted to be a classical artist like Rembrandt, da Vinci, and other legendary painters. He never wavered in his passion for art. As he walked to school one day, though not in an audible voice, the Lord spoke, "I want you to preach the gospel of Jesus Christ all over the world." My father was terrified. He tried to argue, but the undeniable impression kept coming back.

The struggle with God increased in his senior year of high school. Would he attend seminary, as he knew God wanted, or enroll in an art school? Jimmy Dobson said "no" to God then. Yet, even when it seemed God was silent or absent, God continued to work in my father's life.

There are numerous references in Scripture to men who were called by God for specific purposes but refused. (See Judg. 6 regarding Gideon and Jonah 1 to learn of their initial refusals of God's voice.) When God called Moses to lead the children of Israel out of slavery, he had the audacity to argue with the Holy One of Israel: "Please Lord, I have never been eloquent—either in the past or recently since You have been speaking to Your servant—because I am slow of speech and hesitant in speech" (Ex. 4:10).

Have you ever told God He was being unreasonable when He asked you to do something for Him? What happened?

Read God's response to Moses in Exodus 4:11-14.

A person should be very frightened of telling God what he or she will not do. How terrible to think of the Lord's anger against us and missing the opportunity to be used in His service.

Our story continues—My father was just as headstrong as some of these people in the Bible. He had his way, enrolling in the prestigious Art Institute of Pittsburgh. He turned out to be very talented, graduating at the top of his class. On graduation day, Dad's paintings were atop easels across the platform, each one bearing the #1 designation. As Jimmy was walking down the aisle to receive the honor he had earned, a verse of Scripture echoed in his mind from childhood: "Unless the LORD builds a house, its builders labor over it in vain" (Ps. 127:1).

While we'll discover more details later, the lesson my father was learning was that Jesus does not settle for second place. There was nothing sinful or dishonorable about using the talent God had given him; the problem was, my dad's plans did not include God.

WRITING YOUR PERSONAL STORY

The apostle Paul shared his salvation story many times. (See Acts 22:3-11; 26:2-18.) We should be prepared to share with people about the hope we have in Jesus Christ. (See 1 Pet. 3:15.)

Write your story by responding briefly to a few questions. Come to the next group meeting ready to share with others.

What was your life like before you heard about Jesus Christ and His saving love?

What was the defining moment when God got your attention and invited you to repent of your sin, receive His mercy, and surrender your life to Jesus Christ?

Describe both the circumstances and the people God used to help you see your need for Christ.

After becoming a Christian, how has your relationship with Christ impacted your life?

LEGACY SPOTLIGHT:
CHARLES SPURGEON(1834-1892)

One theologian and scholar referred to Charles H. Spurgeon as "one of evangelical Christianity's immortals."[2] Still known as the "Prince of Preachers" more than a century after his death, Charles Haddon Spurgeon is a model for many believers and ministers today.

Although a faithful pastor for decades, Spurgeon was also a faithful father who cultivated a healthy relationship with his twin sons, Thomas and Charles. As Thomas grew older, he recalled the deeply spiritual leadership of his father. "Family worship was a delightful item of each day's doings. His unstudied comments, and his marvelous prayers, were an inspiration indeed."[3]

Charles Spurgeon's letters display his love for his family. On one occasion, one of his sons, Charles, was about to finish school and prepare for a career. In 1874 Dr. Spurgeon wrote these words to "Charlie":

> I am full of hope about you; and if I feel any anxiety, it is because I love you so well that I want you to be a greater success than other young men. I believe you love the Lord, and that is the main thing; the next is, stick to it.

> Leave childish things once for all, and buckle to the work. It will not be pleasant, and it may even become irksome; but the harder you work, at first, the less you will have to do in later life.

> The times are so pushing that you must put out all your energies; and, above all, you must be careful, and very persevering; and then, with God's blessing, you will soon take a position to which your father and mother can point with pleasure.[4]

Clearly, Spurgeon loved his family. He pointed them to Christ and encouraged them to love God more than anything else. His sons became faithful pastors just like their dad. What a legacy he left!

PERSONAL REFLECTION

• • •

When I married Shirley, I committed myself to her. As the days and years go by, I have fallen even more deeply in love with her. My life has changed because I am in love with Shirley, no longer living just for myself.

When you commit yourself to Jesus, you will be changed as well. And your love for Him should increase as your time with Him goes by. Your motivation to serve and obey Him will not be based in guilt or fear, but in abiding love.

Have you fallen in love with Jesus and committed yourself to Him?

How is your love for Him growing each day?

1. Ed Stetzer, "The Time to Reach People Is Now: Seize the Easter Moment (w/ Stats on Outreach)," *The Exchange* (online), 27 March 2013 [cited 25 June 2014]. Available from the Internet: *http://www.christianitytoday.com*.
2. Quoted in Lewis Drummond, *Spurgeon: Prince of Preachers* (Grand Rapids: Kregel Publications, 1992), 11.
3. Quoted in Larry J. Michael, *Spurgeon on Leadership* (Grand Rapids: Kregel Publications, 2003), 127.
4. Ibid., 128.

WEEK 3
SPECIFIC
CALL

● **START YOUR GROUP TIME** by discussing what
participants discovered in their Reflect homework.

Your story of faith is meant to be shared, so break into groups of two
or three and tell your story.

What are you learning about each other's
faith journey?

How do you feel when you think about God using you
to make a lasting impact on your family?

How can you encourage your spouse, children, and
grandkids to grow as disciples?

Disciples are followers of Jesus who have committed their lives to loving
God, loving people, and serving the world with His love and power.

● **WATCH CLIP 3** from the study DVD and answer the following questions:

For several years, my dad wrestled with God's call to be a minister. After going his own way, he yielded to God's call at a special community revival meeting.

What role did my Uncle Willis play in this decision?

One thing I remember about the moment of decision in my own life was how much my mother and father and other family members supported me. I still recall their prayers, encouraging words, and examples.

What are some intentional ways you show your family the importance you place on a growing relationship with Christ?

In response to God's call on his life, my father took a brave step of faith and never looked back. As a result, God used him to impact thousands of lives.

What could God do through you if you were committed to Him?

Once you and I have embraced the claims of Christ, repented of our sinfulness, and received His grace, leaving a legacy of faith is all about walking in humility and obedience. We can embrace these opportunities to live for Him or we can miss out on what God wants to do through us.

● **CONTINUE YOUR GROUP TIME** with this discussion guide.

> What is one of the best opportunities that has ever come your way?

Maybe an honor as a child opened up some unexplored interests. Perhaps you received an invitation to play a sport or go further academically. Maybe college or career offers changed the direction of your life. No doubt part of what made this opportunity so alluring was the challenge and vision of the goal or the promised final outcome.

A CHALLENGE TO OBEY

Two thousand years ago, before His ascension, Jesus gave His followers the greatest opportunity possible—and He places the same privilege before us. If you and I take His command seriously, obeying and relying on Him, God will use us in ways we could never imagine.

● **READ** the words of Jesus in Matthew 28:18-20. What was Jesus commanding His followers to do?

The clear command was to "make disciples" (v. 19).

> How does one "make" a disciple?

One of the primary ways we make disciples is to teach them everything that He has commanded. (See v. 20.)

What tools have you found effective when helping your family understand and apply Jesus' teachings?

Disciples choose to follow Jesus in every area of life. Just as He told His disciples on earth, He says to us: "I want you to lead others to follow Me in every area of life. I want you to invite them to follow Me as their Savior and leader in all of life."

When you become discouraged or distracted from that mission, how do you get back on track?

At the same time He commands us to teach all things, Jesus promises He will always be with us.

How does this promise motivate you?

TIMOTHY'S FAMILY LEGACY

Paul, who was mentoring young Timothy, knew about the rich legacy of faith in Timothy's family.

● **READ** Paul's heartfelt words to Timothy in 2 Timothy 1:3-5.

Paul recognized a strong spiritual heritage. He had experienced many of the benefits himself. (See v. 3.)

What did he say about Timothy's spiritual legacy?

Timothy's mother Eunice and grandmother Lois demonstrated their faith in a way that shaped Timothy.

● **READ** 2 Timothy 3:15.

Timothy's mother and grandmother planted and poured the Word of God into young Timothy, who learned the sacred Scriptures "from childhood." He was grounded in Scripture, which provided the source of "wisdom for salvation through faith in Christ Jesus."

> How can you help your family know the Bible so well that they build their lives on a firm foundation of faith?

> How are you living out your faith genuinely so that your family sees a faith they want to emulate?

To make a disciple assumes that several things are happening:

1. The first assumption is you are living a life of faith yourself. Integrity builds credibility with your disciple.
2. The second is you are spending time with the person you are discipling. Effective disciple-making is about cultivating the relationship in love and trust.

It's not enough to simply live a life of good works. Everybody, including your family, needs to hear how God's Word applies to their lives.

THIS WEEK'S INSIGHTS
• • •

- A disciple is one who surrenders to Jesus Christ and chooses to follow Him in all areas of life.
- Part of disciple-making is mentoring and equipping others, including our family, to be disciples.
- A spiritual heritage helps establish a strong foundation of faith.
- Leaving a legacy of faith is all about making the most of the opportunities we are given.

How will you make the most of the opportunities God gives you this week?

WRAP UP
• • •

THIS WEEK, commit to pray for your family. Using each of their names, ask God to give them the desire to receive His love and grow in their faith in Christ. Rely on this encouragement from Jesus: "And remember, I am with you always, to the end of the age" (Matt. 28:20).

Father, I pray that my impact on my family will
be Your impact. Give me opportunities to grow
in You and to help others know You better.

● **READ AND COMPLETE** the activities for this section before your next group time. For further insight, read chapters 5 and 6 in *Your Legacy: The Greatest Gift*.

SHOWING AND TELLING CHILDREN ABOUT JESUS

Our story: My father married Myrtle Georgia Dillingham who thought she had married a "starving artist." My parents were not walking with the Lord. When a Shreveport church scheduled a revival meeting, many in the community, including my dad's family—not including him—were interested.

The service had already begun by the time my dad and his brothers filed in. A young woman was singing, and as my dad walked to his seat on the front row, the lyrics of the song resonated in my father's heart. The struggle was over. *All right, Lord,* my dad resolved, *I will do what You want. If you want me to give up my dreams of being an artist and become a preacher, I will do it. I'm tired of running away. You can have me.*

He was weeping by the time he reached the front pew. Prompted by the minister who pointed his finger at Jimmy Dobson, asking him to tell the congregation what the Lord had just said to him, my father turned and told the crowd about yielding his will to the Lord—his first brief "sermon." For the rest of his life, he committed his heart and soul to Jesus Christ.

My dad went home and told his new wife that she had indeed married a preacher and she stood beside her husband in ministry for forty-three years. As soon as my father yielded to the call to preach, God showed him how he could paint and still be obedient to his calling. Our home is decorated with his beautiful paintings, and his works hang in other buildings, including homes and churches. Nothing was wasted.

Because he was unprepared for the ministry, my father prayed continually. Some days he spent three to five hours alone with God and the Lord led him through many challenges. As you can imagine, I learned to pray before I learned to talk. I imitated the sounds of my parents' prayers before I knew the meaning of their words.

One Sunday night when I was four, I was sitting by my mother at the back of the church. I remember the events of that evening as though they were yesterday. Dad preached the sermon and asked if there were any who wanted to come forward and give their hearts to the Lord. Without asking my mother, I joined others who were responding. I still remember crying and asking Jesus to forgive me and make me His child. My father stepped down from the platform and came alongside me to pray.

What I did on that night was not manipulated or coerced. It was my choice and I remember feeling so clean. I have tried to please the Lord from that day to this.

After college, I was accepted into the graduate school of the University of Southern California. Seven years later, I finished a PhD in child development and research design, and was offered a position on the medical staff of Children's Hospital of Los Angeles. For fourteen years I was a professor of pediatric medicine at USC School of Medicine.

In 1959, at age 21, the path I would take was beginning to come together. As much as I enjoyed academia, I became increasingly concerned about the institution of the family, which was starting to unravel. Without sounding like a self-appointed prophet, I saw clearly where the nation was headed, anticipating the collapse of marriage, the murder of unborn babies, and the abandonment of biblical morals.

Though I am not a minister, my ultimate objective has been to introduce people to Jesus Christ and to do it through the institution of the family. When I considered the call to preach, as did every other member of my family, I believe the Lord answered with a unique ministry that He has blessed.

How is God tapping and maximizing the gifts He has given you for ministry?

LEGACY SPOTLIGHT: JONATHAN EDWARDS (1703-1758)

Perhaps American history's greatest theologian, Jonathan Edwards, graduated from Yale at the age of 17 and eventually became president of what is now Princeton University. He and his wife, Sarah, had eleven children. Edwards, whose grandfather and father were pastors, also left an unmistakable legacy of faith.

Alvin Reid, professor at Southeastern Baptist Theological Seminary, explains: "The legacy left by the Edwards family demonstrates the effect of a gospel-centered home. More than 400 descendants of Jonathan and Sarah Edwards have been traced. Of these, fourteen became college presidents, roughly one hundred became professors, another one hundred ministers, and about the same number became lawyers or judges. Nearly sixty became doctors, and others were authors or editors."[1]

Jonathan Edwards did not want his children to waste their lives. In 1755, his nine year-old son, Jonathan Jr., was about 200 miles away on a mission trip among the Indians. He wrote a compassionate letter to his son, urging him to seek God and always be ready for eternity:

Dear Child:

Though you are a great way off from us, yet you are not out of our minds: I am full of concern for you, often think of you, and often pray for you. Though you are at so great a distance from us, and from your all your relations, yet this is a comfort to us, that the same God that is here is also at Onohoquaha and that though you are out of our sight, and out of our reach, you are always in God's hands, who is infinitely gracious; and we can go to Him, and commit you to His care and mercy. Take heed that you don't forget or neglect Him. Always set God before your eyes, and live in His fear, and seek Him every day with all diligence: for He, and He only can make you happy or miserable as He pleases; and your Life and Health, and the eternal salvation of your soul and your all in this life and that which is to come depends on His will and pleasure.

The week before last, on Thursday, David died; whom you knew and used to play with, and who used to live at our house. His soul is gone into the eternal world. Whether he was prepared for death, we don't know. This is a loud call of God to you to prepare for death. You see that they that are young die, as well as those that are old; David was not very much older than you. Remember what Christ said, that you must be born again, or you never can see the Kingdom of God. Never give yourself any rest unless you have good evidence that you are converted and become a new creature.

We hope that God will preserve your life and health, and return you to Stockbridge again in safety; but always remember that life is uncertain; you know not how soon you must die, and therefore had need to be always ready. We have very lately heard from your brothers and sisters at Northhampton and at Newark, that they are well. Your aged grandfather and grandmother, when I was at Windsor gave their love to you. We here all do the same.

I am, your tender and affectionate father,

Jonathan Edwards[2]

To leave a legacy like Jonathan Edwards left, we must commit our families to God's care and to continually fear the Lord. And we must remind them about the need to prepare for eternity. By God's grace and in His power, we can build a legacy of faith that lasts forever.

PERSONAL REFLECTION

• • •

Spend some time reflecting on how the first disciples must have felt when Jesus commissioned them. (See Acts 1:7,8.) Imagine yourself in their place, and record your thoughts as a prayer of praise.

Jesus gave these first followers the greatest opportunity in the world, but it was their move. Thankfully, they *did* move. They could have stood still or thought, *Come on, Jesus. That's impossible. Make disciples? The ends of the earth? Are you serious? That's too dangerous.*

But His words, "I am with you always," motivated them to saturate their families and communities with the gospel. Certainly, these words should compel us to do whatever it takes to make disciples.

Disciple-makers take great comfort in knowing that they don't fulfill the mission alone. God is with us. He gives us the strength, energy, ability, and power to do whatever He has asks us to do. Because He is always with us, we should be radical risk-takers.

1. Alvin Reid, "Jonathan and Sarah Edwards: A Legacy of Faith," *AlvinReid.com* (online), 8 January 2007 [cited 25 June 2014]. Available from the Internet: *http://alvinreid.com/?p=199*.
2. Iain H. Murray, *Jonathan Edwards: A New Biography* (Edinburgh, UK: The Banner of Truth Trust, 1987), 394-95.

ETERNITY
BECKONS

· ·

● **START YOUR GROUP TIME** by discussing what participants discovered in their Reflect homework.

> As a child, what family stories did you love hearing over and over again?

> How much do you know about the people who make up your family history? Has this study prompted you to find out more?

> Who in your family lineage lived a life worth emulating? What was it about them that you seek to live out?

> What are you doing that helps you continue to focus on the Lord?

● **WATCH CLIP 4** from the study DVD and answer the following questions:

As you can imagine, the day "Pistol Pete" Maravich died was one that impacted me forever.

> **In times of personal tragedy, how has God shown Himself to you?**

As I talked with the media about Pistol Pete's death, I was able to say with total confidence that Jesus Christ, not basketball, was the greatest love of his life.

> **As you look at another person's life, how can you tell what he or she really loves?**

> **As legacy builders, how can we focus more on the things that matter most?**

People often become passionate about issues that do not last or matter in the long term. Do you recall what I told my seventeen-year-old son, Ryan, when I got home that tragic day? "Be there on that resurrection morning, Ryan, just be there. While you're in the process of doing all the things that seem to matter—you're going to have a family and a job—this outranks everything else, I'll be looking for you, and we will celebrate throughout eternity."

● **CONTINUE YOUR GROUP TIME** with this discussion guide.

Being overly focused on this life has consequences, according to Jesus.

● **READ** John 12:25.

> What did Jesus mean when He said that we must lose our lives and hate this world to have eternal life?

We have a few short years on earth, and then we move on to spend eternity somewhere.

● **READ** Psalm 90:10 and James 4:14.

> How would people live differently if they thought more about the brevity of this life and the length of eternity?

God is looking for people who will step up and say, "I'm ready to help change the world. I'm willing to make a difference in my family." Joshua and Isaiah were two biblical heroes who stepped up and answered the call.

JOSHUA, COURAGEOUS LEADER

At the end of his life, Joshua, the leader of God's people, gathered all Israel and their leaders together for his final challenge. Joshua reminded the people how much God had done for them, how He had delivered them from their enemies, and how He had kept His promises. Then, Joshua issued a passionate charge.

● **READ** Joshua 24:14-15.

What decision did Joshua challenge the Israelites to make? What decision did he make?

No matter what anyone else said or did, Joshua was determined to make the right choice for himself and his family. He knew they would have to live with whatever decision they made. If they chose to serve other gods, they would have to live with that horrible decision and its consequences.

● **READ** Joshua 24:16-25.

What did the people decide?

Certainly Joshua set an example worth following.

As Christ followers wanting to leave a legacy of faith, how do we set a godly example others want to follow?

What difference would it make if more families in your community decided to serve God and God alone?

ISAIAH, PROPHET OF HOPE

Isaiah was a prophet who lived seven hundred years before Christ. Despite all that God had done for them, many of the people in Isaiah's day had rebelled against God. Isaiah devoted his life to telling everyone that there was hope, forgiveness, and joy for anyone who surrendered to God.

Isaiah knew this from personal experience. He came to a point in his life when he knew it was time to surrender.

● **READ** Isaiah 6:1-8.

The world around Isaiah looked bleak. The king had died, and the nation lacked leadership and political stability. Moral and spiritual decay was increasing. Isaiah's vision came just in time. He was reminded that God is in control and is still on His throne.

How does our view of God affect what we do?

As soon as Isaiah realized how holy and great and glorious God was, he realized how sinful he was in comparison.

How does our view of ourselves influence our attitudes and actions?

Isaiah did not say: "Here I am on Sunday." or "Here I am when I have time." or "Here I am when I get older." or "Here I am when I have enough money." Isaiah said, "Here I am! Send me." His words were words of absolute surrender. The prophet was basically saying: "Lord, I know You have a purpose for my life. So I am all Yours. Use me however You want to use me."

THIS WEEK'S INSIGHTS

• • •

- Too often people are passionate about matters that do not last or matter in light of eternity.
- All that we do and say begins to change when we begin living from the perspective of eternity.
- God is looking for people who will step up and say, "I'm ready to help change the world. I'm willing to make a difference in my family. I'm willing to surrender to You."

What will it take for you to step up to this challenge?

WRAP UP

• • •

THIS WEEK, as you conclude this study, spend time as a group praying for three things to happen:

1. For God to lead you to focus on His eternal purposes and to turn your thoughts away from trivial pursuits;
2. For you and your family to demonstrate a Joshua-like commitment to serve God alone;
3. For all families represented by this group to commit daily to obey Jesus' words in Matthew 6:33: "Seek first the kingdom of God and His righteousness."

Heavenly Father, help us to put into practice all that we
have learned from You and about You. As this study
ends, may our service continue and grow. Amen.

● **READ AND COMPLETE** the activities for this section before your next group time. For further insight, read *Your Legacy: The Greatest Gift*, chapters 7-9 and Appendix 2, which includes "Stories for Leaving Your Legacy" to help children understand about Jesus as Savior and Friend.

GIFTS I RECEIVED, LESSONS I'M PASSING ON

from Wanting to Believe: Faith, Family, and Finding an Exceptional Life *by Ryan Dobson (B&H Publishing Group)*

In 1986 I was sixteen and, like many other sixteen-year-olds, I was convinced I knew all the answers. That summer my parents offered me the opportunity to attend a Christian camp, as they had in previous summers. This time I agreed, though reluctantly. I realized within three hours of my two-week experience that my safe, secure world was being totally rocked. Camp organizers had flown in the best minds in Christian scholarship to teach us about Christology and ecclesiology, history and sociology, psychology and anthropology, and other -ologies of which I had never heard. Here they weren't teaching me answers; they were teaching me *how to think.*

I came home from camp a different person. For the first time in my young life, I was becoming me—distinctly, definitely (sometimes defiantly) me. I think this was my dad's goal all along. He wasn't going to spend his parenting chats on hair color or tattoos or clothes; no, he would save those for one key thing: What did I make of the truth?

He was determined to know truth for himself, to enjoy living in light of that truth, and then to expose me to that bright light. He then was committed to standing back and watching what I did with it: Would it arrest me? Change me? Penetrate the tall walls I had built?

The gift my dad gave me was to provide enough rope to either hang myself, or else to knot myself to an anchor that would weather every one of life's storms. Of course that anchor is Jesus, and wisely, I chose that route.

Nearly eight years ago, we welcomed our first child, Lincoln, into our world. We had so hoped my parents would be present when Laura went into labor, but Dad was in Nashville—about to go on stage for his talk just as Lincoln was being born. When I finally got through to Dad, we shared a few laughs and tears and then I knew he had to go. People who were in attendance at that talk told me that he opened his remarks by bounding onto the stage, puffing out his chest, and proclaiming, "Ladies and gentlemen, exactly sixty seconds ago, I became a grandfather for the very first time," to which the crowd unabashedly roared and cheered.

I look at Lincoln today—he's seven, going on eight—and I think, *You don't fully know it yet, but you are ridiculously blessed. To have God put you in this lineage, in a family that will love you this well ... you're more blessed than you know.*

I wonder what his life's trajectory will be—the places he'll go, the decisions he'll make, the person he will someday become—and I praise God that I was raised by a dad who majors in the majors and lets the minors unfold as they may. Lincoln has high highs and low lows and is gutsy and artistic and smart—in a thousand ways he is just like me, but in thousands more, he's his own man.

He loves team sports, which is a little amusing to his anti-team-sports dad. I've always gravitated toward skating, surfing, wrestling, fighting—things you can compete in on your own—but since my son is into baseball, I now am into baseball. I'm into baseball because I'm into *him*. It's a lesson I learned from my dad.

As it relates to my kids—Lincoln and little Luci too—I've decided that wherever they go and whatever they do, however they live and whomever they love, I will do my very best to keep my heart and my arms wide open, always eager to welcome in these two I totally adore.

STRATEGIES FOR LEAVING YOUR LEGACY

Many parents are looking for practical ideas for spiritual training for their children. Just as I hope you are blessed with godly friends who support your family, so are Shirley and I grateful to Robert and Bobbie Wolgemuth for their friendship and expertise with children. Some of these concepts come from their book *How to Lead Your Child to Christ*.

PROVIDE BIBLES FOR EVERY FAMILY MEMBER, EVEN THE YOUNGEST CHILD. At night when you tuck your children into bed, read to them from *their* Bible. If they are old enough, ask them to read with you. Teach them, at the earliest age, that the path to obedience is paved with truth from God's Word.

TEACH YOUR CHILDREN TO MEMORIZE SCRIPTURE. Young children are learning rapidly, and the verses they learn now may last their entire lives. Teach a passage by having children write it on a card and repeat it, phrase by phrase. As a family, work on Scripture memory in the car or at the dinner table. Turn it into a game.

TEACH THEM TO PRAY. USE TABLE TALK AND OTHER DAILY OPPORTUNITIES. Mealtimes and bedtime are natural times to pray. Children like to pray for people (and pets) and to thank God. Guide them also to ask God to forgive them for certain actions. As you voice words of adoration, confess your sins, make specific requests, and thank Him for listening—they too will learn how to pray.

SING TOGETHER. You will be surprised at how quickly children enjoy and learn through music. Spiritual truths are impressed on their hearts and minds as they sing and as you sing as a family.

CONNECT WITH A LOCAL CHURCH. Another way children learn to worship and honor Christ is through worship and Bible study each week. They learn to worship as a family and develop a bond with Christ, His family of believers, and with you. They learn how to apply

God's Word to their lives from the youngest age to participating as a young adult on the mission field.

PASS ON YOUR FAITH. The best way to begin a conversation about your children receiving the gift of God's grace is to tell them about your own faith journey. Remind them:

- How great and good their Heavenly Father is and how much He loves them
- How they need Jesus to forgive them
- How Jesus' death on the cross and His resurrection from the grave can save them from their sin and Satan's power over them, and can bring them into a lifelong friendship with God
- That Jesus loves them so much that He wants to show them how to live with Him both now and forever

BE A PART OF YOUR CHILD'S PRAYING TO RECEIVE CHRIST AND CELEBRATE TOGETHER. You cannot accept Jesus for your children, but you can help them understand how to grab hold of salvation once they recognize their need. Allow the Holy Spirit to use you and His Word to communicate actions and attitudes for coming to God in faith. Whether you help with specific words or assist a child in praying for himself or herself, listen for sincere words of gratitude, repentance, an acknowledgment of God's grace, and acceptance and thanks for His promises.

Even the angels rejoiced when people acknowledged Him so why not mark the occasion with a family celebration? Let the child tell his grandparents this good news. Buy a new Bible and record the child's spiritual birth date. Let her choose a special place to eat.

Which strategy will you begin to use with your family?

LEGACY SPOTLIGHT:
JOHN PIPER (BORN 1946)

John Piper, a pastor for more than 30 years, preached a tribute to his father on Father's Day 2005 based on eleven truths—only "a fragment of the legacy of truth imparted to me by my father."

1. There is a great, majestic God in heaven, and we were meant to live for His glory. (See 1 Cor. 10:31.)
2. When things don't go the way they should, God always makes them turn for good. (See Rom. 8:28.)
3. God can be trusted. (See Prov. 3:5-6; Phil. 4:19.)
4. Life is precarious, and life is precious. Don't presume that you will have it tomorrow and don't waste it today. (See Heb. 9:27.)
5. A merry heart does good like a medicine and Christ is the great Heart-Satisfier. (See Prov. 17:22.)
6. A Christian is a great doer, not a great don'ter. (See Eccl. 9:10; Jas. 1:22.)
7. The Christian life is supernatural. (See John 3:7.)
8. Bible doctrine is important but don't beat people up with it. (See Eph. 4:15.)
9. Respect your mother. (See Deut. 5:16.)
10. Be who God made you to be and not somebody else. (See Rom. 12:6.)
11. People are lost and need to be saved through faith in Jesus Christ. (See Rom. 6:23.)[1]

PERSONAL REFLECTION
• • •

Record a few "takeaways" from this four-week journey and share them with your family.

1. John Piper, "Fathers, Bring Them Up in the Discipline & Instruction of the Lord," *Desiring God* (online), 19 June 2005 [cited 25 June 2014]. Available from the Internet: *http://www.desiringgod.org*.

Key Insights

WEEK 1

- A person with faith like Abraham's is fully convinced that God will accomplish what He has promised.
- Abraham obeyed God and God blessed him beyond expectation.
- In his obedience, Abraham gave glory to God and helped establish a legacy of faith for future generations.
- God continues to bless and use people of faith to bless others and give glory to Him.

WEEK 2

- There is a difference between religion and a personal faith relationship with Jesus.
- Only God can change hearts; we cannot change ourselves.
- When we fully surrender to Jesus Christ, He produces life change in our decisions and our relationships.
- God also seeks to change us as we walk daily in faith.

WEEK 3

- A disciple is one who surrenders to Jesus Christ and chooses to follow Him in all areas of life.
- Part of disciple-making is mentoring and equipping others, including our family, to be disciples.
- A spiritual heritage helps establish a strong foundation of faith.
- Leaving a legacy of faith is all about making the most of the opportunities we are given.

WEEK 4

- Too often people are passionate about matters that do not last or matter in light of eternity.
- All that we do and say begins to change when we begin living from the perspective of eternity.
- God is looking for people who will step up and say, "I'm ready to help change the world. I'm willing to make a difference in my family. I'm willing to surrender to You."

Leader Notes

It's time for a leadership adventure. Don't worry; you don't have to have all the answers. Your role is to facilitate the group discussion, getting participants back on topic when they stray, encouraging everyone to share honestly and authentically, and guiding those who might dominate the conversation to make sure others are also getting some time to share.

As facilitator, take time to look over this entire study guide, noting the order and requirements of each session. Watch all the videos as well. Take time to read the suggested chapters (noted in the beginning of each Reflect section) from the book *Your Legacy: The Greatest Gift* (ISBN 978-1-4555-7343-1). And pray over the material, the prospective participants, and your time together.

You have the option of extending your group's study by showing the film *Your Legacy*. You can also keep it to four weeks by using just this study guide and DVD. The study is easy to customize for your group's needs.

Go over the How to Use This Study and the Guidelines for Groups sections with participants, making everyone aware of best practices and the steps of each session. Then dive into Week 1.

In establishing a schedule for each group meeting, consider ordering these elements for the hour of time together:

1. Connect—10 minutes
2. Watch—15 minutes
3. Engage—35 minutes

Be sure to allow time during each session to show the video clip. All four clips are approximately eight minutes or less in length. Reflect refers to the home study or activities done between group sessions.

Beginning with session 2, encourage some sharing regarding the previous week's Reflect home study. Usually at least one Connect question allows for this interaction. Sharing about the previous week's activities encourages participants to study on their own and be ready to share with their group during the next session.

As the study comes to a close, consider some ways to keep in touch. There may be some additional studies for which group members would like information. Some may be interested in knowing more about your church.

Occasionally, a group member may have needs that fall outside the realm of a supportive small group. If someone would be better served by the pastoral staff at your church or a professional counselor, please maintain a list of professionals to privately offer to that person, placing his/her road to recovery in the hands of a qualified pastor or counselor.

Use the space below to make notes or to identify specific page numbers and questions you would like to discuss with your small group each week based on their needs and season of life.

Further Resources

Need more guidance? Check out the following for help.

ON PARENTING:
The New Dare to Discipline by Dr. James Dobson
The New Strong-Willed Child by Dr. James Dobson
Bringing Up Boys by Dr. James Dobson
Bringing Up Girls by Dr. James Dobson
Dr. Dobson's Handbook of Family Advice by Dr. James Dobson
Night Light for Parents by Dr. James Dobson
Parenting Isn't for Cowards by Dr. James Dobson
Raising Boys and Girls by Sissy Goff, David Thomas, and Melissa Trevathan
Love No Matter What by Brenda Garrison
Intentional Parenting by Sissy Goff, David Thomas, and Melissa Trevathan
Raising Girls by Melissa Trevathan and Sissy Goff
The Back Door to Your Teen's Heart by Melissa Trevathan
5 Love Languages by Gary Chapman
5 Conversations You Must Have with Your Daughter by Vicki Courtney
Parenting Teens magazine
HomeLife magazine
ParentLife magazine
The Parent Adventure by Selma and Rodney Wilson
Experiencing God at Home by Richard Blackaby and Tom Blackaby
Love Dare for Parents by Stephen Kendrick and Alex Kendrick
Authentic Parenting in a Postmodern Culture by Mary E. DeMuth
Grace-Based Parenting by Tim Kimmel
The Most Important Place on Earth by Robert Wolgemuth

ON DISCUSSING FAITH WITH YOUR CHILDREN:
Bringing the Gospel Home by Randy Newman
Firsthand by Ryan Shook and Josh Shook
God Distorted by John Bishop
Sticky Faith by Dr. Kara E. Powell and Dr. Chap Clark
Parenting Beyond Your Capacity by Reggie Joiner and Carey Nieuwhof
A Praying Life by Paul Miller
Faith Conversations for Families by Jim Burns

Introducing Your Child to Christ

Your most significant calling and privilege as a parent is to introduce your children to Jesus Christ. A good way to begin this conversation is to tell them about your own faith journey.

Outlined below is a simple gospel presentation you can share with your child. Define any terms they don't understand and make it more conversational, letting the Spirit guide your words and allowing your child to ask questions and contribute along the way.

GOD RULES. The Bible tells us God created everything, and He's in charge of everything. (See Gen. 1:1; Col. 1:16-17; Rev. 4:11.)

WE SINNED. We all choose to disobey God. The Bible calls this sin. Sin separates us from God and deserves God's punishment of death. (See Rom. 3:23; 6:23.)

GOD PROVIDED. God sent Jesus, the perfect solution to our sin problem, to rescue us from the punishment we deserve. It's something we, as sinners, could never earn on our own. Jesus alone saves us. (See John 3:16; Eph. 2:8-9.)

JESUS GIVES. He lived a perfect life, died on the cross for our sins, and rose again. Because Jesus gave up His life for us, we can be welcomed into God's family for eternity. This is the best gift ever! (See Rom. 5:8; 2 Cor. 5:21; Eph. 2:8-9; 1 Pet. 3:18.)

WE RESPOND. Believe in your heart that Jesus alone saves you through what He's already done on the cross. Repent, by turning away from your sin. Tell God and others that your faith is in Jesus. (See John 14:6; Rom. 10:9-10,13.)

If your child is ready to respond, explain what it means for Jesus to be Lord of his or her life. Guide your child to a time in prayer to repent and express his or her belief in Jesus. If your child responds in faith, celebrate! You now have the opportunity to disciple your child to be more like Christ.

BUILD YOUR FAMILY LEGACY.

Dr. James Dobson leads you through his classic messages and new insights for today's families in these eight DVD-based Bible studies. Each Building a Family Legacy Bible study includes four-sessions with personal reflection and discussion guides along with a DVD of Dr. Dobson's teachings, introduced by his son, Ryan. Studies include:

Your Legacy Bible Study
Bringing Up Boys Bible Study
Bringing Up Girls Bible Study
Dare to Discipline Bible Study
The Strong-Willed Child Bible Study
Straight Talk to Men Bible Study
Love for a Lifetime Bible Study
Wanting to Believe Bible Study

Learn more at LifeWay.com/Legacy

Dr. James Dobson's **BUILDING A FAMILY LEGACY** campaign includes films, Bible studies, and books designed to help families of all ages and stages. Dr. Dobson's wisdom, insight, and humor promise to strengthen marriages and help parents meet the remarkable challenges of raising children. Most importantly, **BUILDING A FAMILY LEGACY** will inspire parents to lead their children to personal faith in Jesus Christ.

Learn more at

BUILDINGAFAMILYLEGACY.COM

More Building a Family Legacy Resources

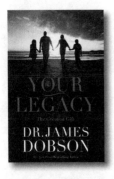

YOUR LEGACY • DR. JAMES DOBSON

Whatever stage you are in as a parent or grandparent, you can leave a spiritual legacy that will equip your children and grandchildren with an unshakable heritage of faith. *Your Legacy* tells you how by presenting Dr. Dobson's personal story of his own spiritual legacy, strategies for the spiritual training of children, and much more.
978-1-4555-7343-1 (FaithWords)

WANTING TO BELIEVE • RYAN DOBSON

When it comes to life, we want to get it right. In *Wanting to Believe*, Ryan Dobson lays out fifteen everyday proverbs passed from sensible parents to a stubborn son and discloses all the ways he tried to refute them, before finding them reliable in the end.
978-1-4336-8252-0 (B&H Publishing Group)

DON'T MISS THE
BUILDING A FAMILY LEGACY 8-DVD series!

Building on highlights from Dr. Dobson's historic first film series, BUILDING A FAMILY LEGACY adds new footage from his lifetime of experience and learning, filmed before standing-room-only audiences. The eight sessions are *Your Legacy, Bringing Up Boys, Bringing Up Girls, Love for a Lifetime, The Strong-Willed Child, Dare to Discipline, Straight Talk to Men,* and *Wanting to Believe* (with Ryan Dobson), plus bonus features!